P9-AQM-368

WITHDRAWN

6

very
young
VERSES

Selected by
Barbara Peck Geismer
and
Antoinette Brown Suter

Illustrated by
Mildred Bronson

66869

Houghton Mifflin Company
Boston
The Riverside Press Cambridge

Cody Memorial Library
Southwestern University
Georgetown, Texas

COPYRIGHT, 1945, BY HOUGHTON MIFFLIN COMPANY

ALL RIGHTS RESERVED INCLUDING THE RIGHT TO REPRODUCE
THIS BOOK OR PARTS THEREOF IN ANY FORM

The Riverside Press
CAMBRIDGE · MASSACHUSETTS
PRINTED IN THE U.S.A.

C
808.81
G277v

TO
OUR CHILDREN

FOREWORD

THE idea for the present anthology was conceived in the course of our work together as teachers at Shady Hill School in Cambridge, Massachusetts. Each of us had discovered the need for a compact and readily available source of poems for use with children under six. Individually we had started small and limited collections of verses that had proved successful with very young children. While teaching together at Shady Hill we realized that our purpose could best be accomplished by combining our collections and compiling a single volume which would contain a well-balanced selection from the works of recognized poets whose works deal with the things closest to little children.

Together and independently we have experimented with a large variety of poems and used them with both individuals and groups. We have been careful to watch for the children's responses and enthusiasms. For some children this was their first introduction to poetry and it was exciting to see how general its appeal was to them. Their reasons for asking to have certain poems read and re-read were as numerous as their interests in their surroundings were varied.

In making a final selection of verses to be included in this anthology we have chosen those which have proved to have the greatest appeal, either by their content, rhythm, words, sound, or humor. We particularly felt that those poems should be included which stimulated a distinct and lively response. This response appeared in a wide variety of spontaneous reactions: animated discussion of the subject matter, experimentation with novel words and sounds, and new ideas expressed in visual art, musical rhythms and dramatic play.

Two very familiar groups of poems which children love, and which certainly should be on the book-shelf and part of every child's story time, are not represented in this collection — *Mother Goose* and the poetry of A. A. Milne. *Mother Goose* can be obtained in many inexpensive editions and is accessible to everyone; A. A. Milne's poems are not at present available for reprinting.

Our hope is that this anthology will enable little children to enjoy poetry with grownups. We have had reassuring encouragement from many parents and teachers, our publisher, and of most importance, from successful use with a great number of children. It would be impossible to mention them all by name, but we are very grateful for their help and interest.

BARBARA PECK GEISMER
ANTOINETTE BROWN SUTER

CONTENTS

BIRDS, BEASTS, AND BUGS

ABOUT ME

ABOUT OTHER PEOPLE AND THINGS

ABOUT GOING PLACES

ABOUT THE SEASONS

ABOUT THE WEATHER

JUST PRETEND

JUST FOR FUN

PRAYERS

birds
beasts
and bugs

JUMP OR JIGGLE

Frogs jump
Caterpillars hump

Worms wiggle
Bugs jiggle

Rabbits hop
Horses clop

Snakes slide
Seagulls glide

Mice creep
Deer leap

Puppies bounce
Kittens pounce

Lions stalk —
But —
I walk!

THE GOLDFISH

My darling little goldfish
Hasn't any toes;
He swims around without a sound
And bumps his hungry nose.

He can't get out to play with me,
Nor I get in to him,
Although I say: "Come out and play,"
And he — "Come in and swim."

LITTLE SNAIL

I saw a snail
Come down the garden walk,
He wagged his head this way . . . that way . . .
Like a clown in the circus.
He looked from side to side
As though he were from a different country.
I have always said he carried his house on his back . . .
Today in the rain
I saw that it was his umbrella!

THE SNAIL

The snail is very odd and slow.
He has his mind made up to go
The longest way to anywhere
And will not let you steer him there.

Today I met one in the grass
And hadn't time to watch him pass,
But coming back at sunset, I
Discovered him still traveling by.

The grass-blades grew so thick and tall
I asked him why he climbed them all,
And told him I had sometimes found
The shortest way was going 'round.

He was not easy to persuade,
To judge by any sign he made,
And when I lectured him some more
Went in his house and shut the door.

REGENT'S PARK

What makes the ducks in the pond, I wonder, go
Suddenly under?

Down they go in the neatest way;
You'd be surprised at the time they stay,
You stand on the bank and you wait and stare,
Trying to think what they do down there;
And, just as you're feeling anxious, then
Suddenly up they come again,
Ever so far from where you guessed,
Dry and tidy and self-possessed.

What is it makes the duck, I wonder, go
Suddenly under?

THE LITTLE TURTLE

There was a little turtle.
He lived in a box.
He swam in a puddle.
He climbed on the rocks.

He snapped at a mosquito.
He snapped at a flea.
He snapped at a minnow.
And he snapped at me.

He caught the mosquito.
He caught the flea.
He caught the minnow.
But he didn't catch me.

GRANDFATHER FROG

Fat green frog sits by the pond,
Big frog, bull frog, grandfather frog.
Croak-croak-croak.
Shuts his eye, opens his eye,
Rolls his eye, winks his eye,
Waiting for
A little fat fly.
Croak, croak.
I go walking down by the pond,
I want to see the big green frog,
I want to stare right into his eye,
Rolling, winking, funny old eye.
But oh! he hears me coming by.
Croak-croak —
SPLASH!!

GOOD MORNING

One day I saw a downy duck,
With feathers on his back;
I said, "Good morning, downy duck,"
And he said, "Quack, quack, quack."

One day I saw a timid mouse,
He was so shy and meek;
I said, "Good morning, timid mouse,"
And he said, "Squeak, squeak, squeak."

One day I saw a curly dog,
I met him with a bow;
I said, "Good morning, curly dog,"
And he said, "Bow-wow-wow."

One day I saw a scarlet bird,
He woke me from my sleep;
I said, "Good morning, scarlet bird,"
And he said, "Cheep, cheep, cheep."

UNDER THE GROUND

What is under the grass,
Way down in the ground,
Where everything is cool and wet
With darkness all around?

Little pink worms live there;
Ants and brown bugs creep
Softly round the stones and rocks
Where roots are pushing deep.

Do they hear us walking
On the grass above their heads;
Hear us running over
While they snuggle in their beds?

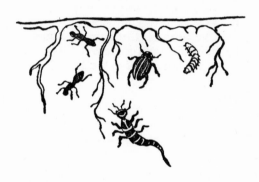

LITTLE BLACK BUG

Little black bug,
Little black bug,
Where have you been?
I've been under the rug,
Said little black bug.
Bug-ug-ug-ug.

Little green fly,
Little green fly,
Where have you been?
I've been way up high,
Said little green fly.
Bzzzzzzzzzzzzzz.

Little old mouse,
Little old mouse,
Where have you been?
I've been all through the house,
Said little old mouse.
Squeak-eak-eak-eak-eak.

LITTLE BUG

A weeny little bug
Goes climbing up the grass,
What a lot of tiny little legs he has!

I can see his eyes,
Small and black and shiny.
I *can't think* how it feels to be so tiny!

THE CRICKET

And when the rain had gone away
And it was shining everywhere,
I ran out on the walk to play
And found a little bug was there.

And he was running just as fast
As any little bug could run,
Until he stopped for breath at last,
All black and shiny in the sun.

And then he chirped a song to me
And gave his wings a little tug,
And *that's* the way he showed that he
Was very glad to be a bug!

"BROWN AND FURRY"

Brown and furry
Caterpillar in a hurry
Take your walk
To the shady leaf, or stalk,
Or what not,
Which may be the chosen spot.
No toad spy you,
Hovering bird of prey pass by you;
Spin and die,
To live again a butterfly.

"FUZZY WUZZY, CREEPY CRAWLY"

Fuzzy wuzzy, creepy crawly
   Caterpillar funny,
You will be a butterfly
   When the days are sunny.

Winging, flinging, dancing, springing
   Butterfly so yellow,
You were once a caterpillar,
   Wiggly, wiggly fellow.

AN EXPLANATION OF THE GRASSHOPPER

The Grasshopper, the Grasshopper,
I will explain to you: —
He is the Brownies' racehorse,
The fairies' kangaroo.

THE DRUMMER

Rat-a-tat-tat . . .
See Bunny come
Sporting green breeches
And rolling his drum.

Rat-a-tat-tat . . .
Little pink nose
Must have been snooping
Into a rose.

Rat-a-tat-tat . . .
Rabbit, the drummer,
Straightens his ear
And marches with summer.

RABBITS

My two white rabbits
Chase each other
With humping, bumping backs.
  They go hopping, hopping,
  And their long ears
    Go flopping, flopping.
          And they
          Make faces
          With their noses
          Up and down.

Today
I went inside their fence
To play rabbit with them.
And in one corner
Under a loose bush
I saw something shivering the leaves.
And I pushed
And looked.
And I found —
There
In a hole
In the ground —
Three baby rabbits
Hidden away.
          And *they*
          Made faces
          With their noses
          Up and down.

"THE CITY MOUSE LIVES IN A HOUSE"

The city mouse lives in a house; —
    The garden mouse lives in a bower,
He's friendly with the frogs and toads,
    And sees the pretty plants in flower.

The city mouse eats bread and cheese; —
    The garden mouse eats what he can;
We will not grudge him seeds and stalks.
    Poor little timid furry man.

THE HOUSE OF THE MOUSE

The house of the mouse
is a wee little house,
a green little house in the grass,
which big clumsy folk
may hunt and may poke
and still never see as they pass
this sweet little, neat little,
wee little, green little,
cuddle-down hide-away
house in the grass.

MICE

I think mice
Are rather nice.

> Their tails are long,
> Their faces small,
> They haven't any
> Chins at all.
> Their ears are pink,
> Their teeth are white,
> They run about
> The house at night.
> They nibble things
> They shouldn't touch
> And no one seems
> To like them much.

But *I* think mice
Are nice.

CAT

My cat
Is quiet
She moves without a sound.
Sometimes she stretches herself high and curving
On tiptoe.
Sometimes she crouches low
And creeping.

Sometimes she rubs herself against a chair,
And there
    With a miew and a miew
    And a purrr purrr purrr
    She curls up
    And goes to sleep.

My cat
Lives through a black hole
Under the house.
So one day I
Crawled in after her.
And it was dark
And I sat
And didn't know
Where to go.
And then —
Two yellow-white
Round little lights
Came moving . . . moving . . . toward me.
And there
With a miew and a miew
And a purrr purrr purrr
My cat
Rubbed, soft, against me.

And I knew
The lights
Were MY CAT'S EYES
In the dark.

TIGER–CAT TIM

Timothy Tim was a very small cat
Who looked like a tiger the size of a rat.
There were little black stripes running all over him,
With just enough white on his feet for a trim
On Tiger-cat Tim.

Timothy Tim had a little pink tongue
That was spoon, comb and washcloth all made into one.
He lapped up his milk, washed and combed all his fur,
And then he sat down in the sunshine to purr
Full little Tim.

Timothy Tim had a queer little way
Of always pretending at things in his play.
He caught pretend mice in the grass and the sand
And fought pretend cats when he played with your hand,
Fierce little Tim!

He drank all his milk, and he grew and he grew,
He ate all his meat and his vegetables too,
He grew very big and he grew very fat,
And now he's a lazy old, sleepy old cat,
Timothy Tim!

SUNNING

Old Dog lay in the summer sun
Much too lazy to rise and run.
He flapped an ear
At a buzzing fly
He winked a half opened
Sleepy eye,
He scratched himself
On an itching spot,
As he dozed on the porch
Where the sun was hot.
He whimpered a bit
From force of habit
While he lazily dreamed
Of chasing a rabbit.
But Old Dog happily lay in the sun
Much too lazy to rise and run.

THE PASTURE

I'm going out to clean the pasture spring;
I'll only stop to rake the leaves away
(And wait to watch the water clear, I may):
I shan't be gone long. — You come too.

I'm going out to fetch the little calf
That's standing by the mother.   It's so young,
It totters when she licks it with her tongue.
I shan't be gone long. — You come too.

THE COW

The friendly cow all red and white,
I love with all my heart:
She gives me cream, with all her might,
To eat with apple tart.

She wanders lowing here and there,
And yet she cannot stray,
All in the pleasant open air,
The pleasant light of day:

And blown by all the winds that pass
And wet with all the showers,
She walks among the meadow grass
And eats the meadow flowers.

THE NEW BABY CALF

Buttercup, the cow, had a new baby calf,
          a fine baby calf,
               a strong baby calf,
Not strong like his mother
But strong for a calf,
For *this* baby calf was so *new!*

Buttercup licked him with her strong warm tongue,
Buttercup washed him with her strong warm tongue,
Buttercup brushed him with her strong warm tongue,
       And the new baby calf *liked that!*

The new baby calf took a very little walk,
            a tiny little walk,
               a teeny little walk,
But his long legs wobbled
When he took a little walk,
       And the new baby calf fell down.

Buttercup told him with a low soft "Moo-oo!"
That he was doing very well for one so very new
And she talked very gently, as mother cows do,
       And the new baby calf *liked that!*

The new baby calf took another little walk,
            a little longer walk,
               a little stronger walk,
He walked around his mother and he found the place to
    drink.
And the new baby calf liked *that!*

Buttercup told him with another low moo
That drinking milk from mother was a fine thing to do,

That she had lots of milk for him and for the farmer too,
    And the new baby calf liked *that!*

The new baby calf drank milk every day,
His legs grew so strong that he could run and play,
He learned to eat grass and then grain and hay,
    And the big baby calf grew fat!

MILKING TIME

When supper time is almost come,
But not quite here, I cannot wait,
And so I take my china mug
And go down by the milking gate.

The cow is always eating shucks
And spilling off the little silk;
Her purple eyes are big and soft —
She always smells like milk.

And father takes my mug from me,
And then he makes the stream come out.
I see it going in my mug
And foaming all about.

And when it's piling very high,
And when some little streams commence
To run and drip along the sides,
He hands it to me through the fence.

IF I WERE A LITTLE PIG

If I were a little pig,
I'd have a snubby nose
With two round holes in the end of it,
And what do you suppose?
I'd do the funniest thing with my nose:
I'd root in the mud with the end of it —
If I were a little pig
With a snubby snout for a nose.

If I were a little pig,
I'd have four short little legs
Stuck in my body so fat and round
Like little walking pegs.
I'd trot in the muddiest mud till my legs
Were just as dirty as dirt on the ground,
If I were a little pig
Who trotted on four short legs.

If I were a little pig,
I'd have a curly tail;
I'd laze through endless sunny days
Till I smelled the dinner pail.
Then uff-uff-uff, what a row I'd raise
From my snubby snout to my curled-up tail,
If I were a little pig
With a kinky curly tail.

If I were a little pig,
I'd have a round hump back,
And my cloven hoof in the mud would make
A little cloven track.
I'd have little wiry hairs on my back
And garbage I'd take as if it were cake,
If I were a little pig
With a round fat hump of a back.

If I were a little pig
And smelled there was something to eat,
I'd hunt with my little pink eyes
And grunt till I found the treat;
Then I'd push with my nose and my cloven toes,
I'd push my brother and even my mother.
I'd bunt and I'd grunt,
I'd wallow and swallow,
I'd squeal for my meal,
I'd fight for a bite;
But what would it matter?
I'd get fatter and fatter!
If I were a little pig,
I'd always be wanting to eat!

Now the way a piggy says "Please"
Is to grab whatever he sees;
And if I were a little pig
And not just only me,
I'd look and sound and smell and feel
And act like one, you see.

WORK HORSES

Big strong work horses working every day,
Big strong work horses pulling loads of hay,
Big strong work horses have no time to play,
     Work! — Work! — Work!
Big strong work horses with a wagon full,
Big strong work horses, pull! pull! pull!
     Pull! — Pull! — Pull!

     Big horse, strong horse,
     Pull the plow, pull the plow,
     Pull hard, work hard,
     Plow the garden, plow, plow!
     Big horse, tired horse,
     Stop and rest now.

Big strong work horses plowing up the ground,
Big strong work horses walking round and round,
Big strong work horses going home to lunch,
Eat oats, eating hay, munch! munch! munch!

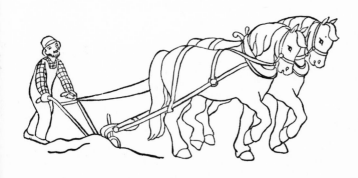

66869

Cody Memorial Library
Southwestern University
Georgetown, Texas

THE ELEPHANT

Here comes the elephant
Swaying along
With his cargo of children
All singing a song:
To the tinkle of laughter
He goes on his way,
And his cargo of children
Have crowned him with may.
His legs are in leather
And padded his toes:
He can root up an oak
With a whisk of his nose:
With a wave of his trunk
And a turn of his chin
He can pull down a house,
Or pick up a pin.
Beneath his gray forehead
A little eye peers;
Of what is he thinking
Between those wide ears?
Of what does he think?
If he wished to tease,
He could twirl his keeper
Over the trees:
If he were not kind,
He could play cup and ball
With Robert and Helen,
And Uncle Paul:
But that gray forehead,
Those crinkled ears,
Have learned to be kind
In a hundred years:
And so with the children
He goes on his way
To the tinkle of laughter
And crowned with the
      may.

CONVERSATION

I called to gray squirrel,
"Good-day, good-day." ...
He flirted his tail
In the friendliest way.

I said to red robin,
"Heigh-o, heigh-o." ...
He stood very straight,
Then bowed very low.

I asked Mistress Tabby,
"Puss, how do you do?"
She purred and she arched,
As she answered, "Mi-eu."

I whistled to Casy,
"Come, hurry, old chap." ...
How he grinned, how he waggled,
And barked his "Yap ... yap!" ...

A LITTLE SQUIRREL

I saw a little squirrel,
Sitting in a tree;
He was eating a nut
And wouldn't look at me.

THE SQUIRREL

Whisky, frisky,
Hippity hop;
Up he goes
To the tree top!

Whirly, twirly,
Round and round,
Down he scampers
To the ground.

Furly, curly
What a tail!
Tall as a feather
Broad as a sail!

Where's his supper?
In the shell,
Snappity, crackity,
Out it fell.

THE BLACKBIRD

In the far corner
Close by the swings,
Every morning
A blackbird sings.

His bill's so yellow,
His coat's so black,
That he makes a fellow
Whistle back.

Ann, my daughter,
Thinks that he
Sings for us two
Especially.

LITTLE LADY WREN

Little Lady Wren,
Hopping from bough to bough,
Bob your tail for me,
Bob it now!

You carry it so straight
Up in the air and when
You hop from bough to bough
You bob it now and then.

Why do you bob your tail,
Hopping from bough to bough,
And will not bob it when I say,
"Bob it now!"?

THE WOODPECKER

The woodpecker pecked out a little round hole,
And made him a house in the telephone pole.
One day when I watched he poked out his head,
And he had on a hood and a collar of red.
When the streams of rain pour out of the sky,
And the sparkles of lightning go flashing by,
And the big, big wheels of thunder roll,
He can snuggle back in the telephone pole.

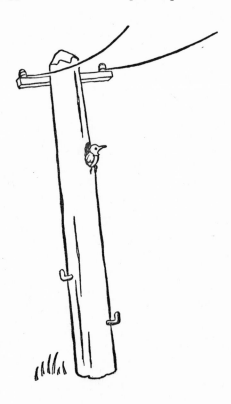

WOODPECKER WITH LONG EARS

The woodpecker there in that tree
Discombobulates me!
He keeps knocking and knocking and knocking till I
Get so angry!   For why
Can't he see
There's no door in that tree?
He knocks all around
From the top to the ground
On the trunk.   Then flies out on a limb.
It's so foolish of him!
If I'd knocked on one tree
As often as he,
I'd make up my mind
There was no door to find.
If I knocked any more
It would be
On some other tree
That might have a door
I could see.

ROBIN

Hop and skip
On the lawn,
Robin Red Breast —
Come and gone.

You skip so fast
Along the ground,
Stop, hop and stop,
Look around.

Hi, spy!
At your feet
A big fat worm!
Sweet to eat!

Bob your head,
Catch him quick!
Pull and haul,
Tug and strain
With might and main,
Gulp and swallow,
That is all.
Very slick!

Skip and hop,
Run and stop,
Look around
On the ground.
Hi, spy!
With might and main
What you did
You do again.

THE ROBIN

When father takes his spade to dig,
Then robin comes along;
He sits upon a little twig,
And sings a little song.

Or, if the trees are very far,
He does not stay alone;
But comes up close to where we are,
And hops upon a stone.

MRS. PECK–PIGEON

Mrs. Peck-Pigeon
Is picking for bread,
Bob-bob-bob
Goes her little round head.
Tame as a pussy cat
In the street,
Step-step-step
Go her little red feet.
With her little red feet
And her little round head,
Mrs. Peck-Pigeon
Goes picking for bread.

about
me

OTHER CHILDREN

Lots of other children
The same size as me.
That's how big I am.

Lots of other children
That are only three.
That's how old I am.

Lots of other children
All around me,
But they aren't me.

They haven't got my mother,
They haven't got my daddy,
And they aren't me!

LITTLE

I am the sister of him
And he is my brother.
He is too little for us
To talk to each other.

So every morning I show him
My doll and my book;
But every morning he still is
Too little to look.

MY ZIPPER SUIT

My zipper suit is bunny-brown —
The toe zips up, the legs zip down.
I wear it every day.
My daddy brought it out from town.
Zip it up, and zip it down,
And hurry out to play.

HAIR RIBBONS

I'm three years old and like to wear,
A bow of ribbon on my hair.
Sometimes it's pink, sometimes it's blue;
I think it's pretty there, don't you?

GROWING UP

My birthday is coming tomorrow,
And then I'm going to be four;
And I'm getting so big that already,
I can open the kitchen door;
I'm very much taller than Baby,
Though today I am still only three;
And I'm bigger than Bob-tail the puppy,
Who used to be bigger than me.

LITTLE BROTHER'S SECRET

When my birthday was coming
Little Brother had a secret.
He kept it for days and days
And just hummed a little tune when I asked him.
But one night it rained.
And I woke up and heard him crying;
Then he told me.
"I planted two lumps of sugar in your garden
Because you love it so frightfully.
I thought there would be a whole sugar tree for your
      birthday.
And now it will be all melted."
Oh, the darling!

FIVE YEARS OLD

Please, everybody, look at me!
Today I'm five years old, you see!
And after this, I won't be four,
Not ever, ever, any more!
I won't be three — or two — or one,
For that was when I'd first begun.
Now I'll be five a while, and then
I'll soon be something else again!

THE MITTEN SONG

"Thumbs in the thumb-place,
Fingers all together!"
This is the song
We sing in mitten weather.
When it is cold,
It doesn't matter whether
Mittens are wool,
Or made of finest leather.
This is the song
We sing in mitten-weather:
"Thumbs in the thumb-place,
Fingers all together!"

Dorothy Aldis

FEET

There are things
Feet know
That hands never will:
The exciting
Pounding feel
Of running down a hill;

The soft cool
Prickliness
When feet are bare
Walking in
The summer grass
To most anywhere.

Or dabbling in
Water all
Slip-sliddering through toes —
(Nicer than
Through fingers, though why
No one really knows.)

"Toes, tell my
Fingers," I
Said to them one day,
"Why it's such
Fun just to
Wiggle and play."

But toes just
Looked at me
Solemn and still.
Oh, there are things
Feet know
That hands NEVER WILL.

HANDS

There are things
Hands do
That feet never can.   Oh
Lots of things
Like stringing beads
Or playing the piano;

Or plaiting little
Stems of grass
Into a little braid
For an acorn
Dolly's head
That somebody has made;

Or shelling slippery
Pods of peas
So the peas can pop;
Or holding things
Quite tightly so
They will not slip or drop.

"Hands, tell my
Toes" I
Said to them one day,
"How you learned
To do so much
More useful things than they."

But hands just
Looked at me
And proudly began:
"Oh, there are things
Hands do
That feet NEVER CAN."

SHOES

My father has a pair of shoes
So beautiful to see!
I want to wear my father's shoes,
They are too big for me.

My baby brother has a pair,
As cunning as can be!
My feet won't go into that pair,
They are too small for me.

There's only one thing I can do
Till I get small or grown.
If I want to have a fitting shoe,
I'll have to wear my own.

NEW SHOES

When I am walking down the street
I do so like to watch my feet.
Perhaps you do not know the news,
Mother has bought me fine new shoes!
When the left one steps I do not speak,
I listen to its happy squeak.

AN INDIGNANT MALE

The way they scrub
Me in the tub,
I think there's
    Hardly
    Any
    Doubt
Sometime they'll rub
And rub and rub
Until they simply
    Rub
    Me
    Out.

NAUGHTY SOAP SONG

Just when I'm ready to
Start on my ears,
That is the time that my
Soap disappears.

It jumps from my fingers and
Slithers and slides
Down to the end of the
Tub, where it hides.

And acts in a most diso-
Bedient way
And THAT'S WHY MY SOAP'S GROWING
THINNER EACH DAY.

WHISTLE

I want to learn to whistle,
I've always wanted to;
I fix my mouth to do it, but,
The whistle won't come through.

I think perhaps it's stuck, and so
I try it once again;
Can people swallow whistles,
Where is my whistle then?

SNEEZING

Air comes in tickly
Through my nose,
Then very quickly —
Out it goes:
Ahhh — CHOO!

With every sneeze
I have to do,
I make a breeze —
Ahh — CHOO! — Ahh — CHOO!

BOUNCING BALL

I wish I had a great big ball
To bounce up to the sky;
I'd bounce it 'til it hit a cloud
That the wind was blowing by.

My ball would strike the cloud so hard
That it would burst in two,
And empty all its store of rain
On me, our house, and you.

MY SHADOW

I have a little shadow that goes in and out with me,
And what can be the use of him is more than I can see.
He is very, very like me from the heels up to the head;
And I see him jump before me, when I jump into my bed.

The funniest thing about him is the way he likes to
    grow —
Not at all like proper children, which is always very
    slow;
For he sometimes shoots up taller like an india rubber
    ball,
And he sometimes gets so little that there's none of him
    at all.

He hasn't got a notion of how children ought to play,
And can only make a fool of me in every sort of way.
He stays so close beside me, he's a coward you can see;
I'd think shame to stick to nursie as that shadow sticks
    to me!

One morning, very early, before the sun was up,
I rose and found the shining dew on every buttercup;
But my lazy little shadow, like an errant sleepyhead,
Had stayed at home behind me and was fast asleep in
    bed.

ANIMAL CRACKERS

Animal crackers, and cocoa to drink,
That is the finest of suppers, I think;
When I'm grown up and can have what I please
I think I shall always insist upon these.

What do YOU choose when you're offered a treat?
When Mother says "What would you like best to eat?"
Is it waffles and syrup, or cinnamon toast?
It's cocoa and animals that *I* love the most!

The kitchen's the cosiest place that I know:
The kettle is singing, the stove is aglow,
And there in the twilight, how jolly to see
The cocoa and animals waiting for me.

Daddy and Mother dine later in state,
With Mary to cook for them, Susan to wait;
But they don't have nearly as much fun as I
Who eat in the kitchen with Nurse standing by;
And Daddy once said, he would like to be me
Having cocoa and animals once more for tea!

MY BED

I have a little bed
Just for me.
Brother's too big for it.
Mummy's too big for it.
Daddy's too big for it.
Do you see?

I have a little bed,
Do you see?
But — pussy's too small for it.
Puppy's too small for it.
Baby's too small for it.
It's just for me.

STARS

Bright stars, light stars
Shining-in-the-night stars,
Little twinkly, winkly stars,
Deep in the sky.

Yellow stars, red stars,
Shine-when-I'm-in-bed stars,
Oh how many blinky stars,
Far, far away!

"SOFTLY, DROWSILY"

Softly, drowsily,
Out of sleep;
Into the world again
Ann's eyes peep;
Over the pictures
Across the walls
One little quivering
Sunbeam falls.
A thrush in the garden
Seems to say,
Wake, Little Ann,
'Tis day, 'tis day;
Faint sweet breezes
The casement stir
Breathing of pinks
And lavender,
At last from her pillow,
With cheeks bright red,
Up comes her round little
Tousled head;
And out she tumbles
From her warm bed.

about
other people
and things

"TALL PEOPLE, SHORT PEOPLE"

Tall people, short people,
Thin people, fat,
Lady so dainty
Wearing a hat.
Straight people, dumpy people,
Man dressed in brown;
Baby in a buggy,
These make a Town.

"I'M THE POLICE COP MAN, I AM"

I'm the police cop man, I am, I am.
Cars can't go till I say they can.
I stand in the middle of the street, I do
And tell them to go when I want them to.
Whizzing taxis and automobiles,
Trotting horses and clattering wheels,
And rumbling, grumbling, huge big trucks
And even the lazy old trolley car
Can't go very far
      When up goes my hand
             and
"Traffic stop," says the traffic cop.
Then many little children's feet
Go hippity across the street.

BARBER'S CLIPPERS

The barber snips and snips
My hair with his scissors
And then he zips on
His clippers.
   It clips
   Up and down
   And around
   My hair in back.

     Ssss ssss
     It swishes
     On the sides
     Behind my ears.

     Ssss ssss
     It tickles
     As it slides
       Straight up the middle
       Of my neck.

THE DENTIST

I'd like to be a dentist with a plate upon the door
And a little bubbling fountain in the middle of the floor;
With lots of tiny bottles all arranged in colored rows
And a page-boy with a line of silver buttons down his
      clothes.

I'd love to polish up the things and put them every day
Inside the darling chests of drawers all tidily away;
And every Sunday afternoon when nobody was there
I should go riding up and down upon the velvet chair.

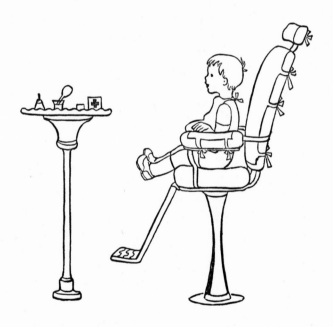

THE COBBLER

Crooked heels
   And scuffy toes
Are all the kinds
   Of shoes he knows.

He patches up
   The broken places,
Sews the seams
   And shines their faces.

THE POSTMAN

Eight o'clock,
The postman's knock!
Five letters for Papa;
    One for Lou,
    And none for you,
And three for dear Mamma.

THE MILKMAN'S HORSE

On summer mornings when it's hot,
The milkman's horse can't even trot;
But pokes along like this —
Klip-klop, Klip-klop, Klip-klop.

But in the winter brisk,
He perks right up and wants to frisk;
And then he goes like this —
Klippty-klip, Klippty-klip, Klippty-klip.

THE MILKMAN

Good luck to the milkman,
He's cold on his cart,
But he whistles a tune
To keep up his heart.
And when we're all sleeping,
Or sleepily drowse,
He's out in the meadows
And milking his cows.

Rhoda W. Bacmeister

MILK IN WINTER

In the early, shivery dark
Of wintertime I wake
And hear the klinkey-klank
That our milk bottles make.

The empty bottles clatter,
Boots on the snow peep-peep,
The milkman's truck goes rumbling off,
And I go back to sleep.

When I get up for breakfast
The morning dark is gone,
But there's the milk outside the door
With tall ice-cream hats on!

THE ICE–CREAM MAN

When summer's in the city,
   And brick's a blaze of heat,
The Ice-Cream Man with his little cart
   Goes trundling down the street.

Beneath his round umbrella,
   Oh, what a joyful sight,
To see him fill the cones with mounds
   Of cooling brown or white:

Vanilla, chocolate, strawberry,
   Or chilly things to drink
From bottles full of frosty-fizz,
   Green, orange, white, or pink.

His cart might be a flower bed
   Of roses and sweet peas,
The way the children cluster round
   As thick as honeybees.

MERRY–GO–ROUND

I climbed up on the merry-go-round,
And it went round and round.

I climbed up on a big brown horse
And it went up and down.

Around and round
And up and down,
Around and round
And up and down.
I sat high up
On a big brown horse
And rode around
On the merry-go-round
And rode around.

On the merry-go-round
I rode around
On the merry-go-round
Around
And round
And round.

LAWN–MOWER

I'm the gardener today.
I push the lawn-mower
Across the grass.
    Zwuzz, wisssh, zwuzz, wisssh.

        I'm the lawn's barber.
        I'm cutting
        Its green hair
           Short.

I push the lawn-mower
Across the grass.
    Zwuzz, wisssh.

SEESAW

Up and down,
Up and down,
Seesaws pop
Up,
Seesaws drop
Down.
The down is a bump,
The up is a jump.
See-saw,
See-saw,
UP!

THE SWING

How do you like to go up in a swing,
  Up in the air so blue?
Oh, I do think it the pleasantest thing
  Ever a child can do!

Up in the air and over the wall,
  Till I can see so wide,
Rivers and trees and cattle and all
  Over the countryside —

Till I look down on the garden green,
  Down on the roof so brown —
Up in the air I go flying again,
  Up in the air and down!

about
going
places

MOVING

I like to move.   There's such a feeling
Of hurrying
    and scurrying,
And such a feeling
Of men with trunks and packing cases,
Of kitchen clocks and mother's laces,
Dusters, dishes, books, and vases,
Toys and pans and candles.

I always find things I'd forgotten:
An old brown Teddy stuffed with cotton,
Some croquet mallets without handles,
A marble and my worn-out sandals,
A half an engine and a hat. . . .
And I like that.

I like to watch the big vans backing,
And the lumbering
    and the cumbering,
And the hammering and the tacking.
I even like the packing.

And that will prove
I like to move!

THERE ARE SO MANY WAYS OF
GOING PLACES

Big yellow trolley lumbers along,
Long black subway sings an under song,
Airplanes swoop and flash in the sky,
Noisy old elevated goes rocketing by.
Boats across the water — back and forth they go,
Big boats and little boats, fast boats and slow.
Trains puff and thunder; their engines have a headlight;
They have a special kind of car where you can sleep all
      night.
Tall fat buses on the Avenue,
They will stop for anyone — even — just — you.
All kinds of autos rush down the street.
And then there are always — your own two feet.

I LISTEN TO THE WHISTLES

I listen to the whistles
From my window on the street.
I listen to the whistles
When it's hard to go to sleep.

I hear the little tugboats
And the ocean liners, too.
The little tugs say chug-a-chug,
And the ocean liners, whoo-oo-oo.

Sometimes I hear a fire engine
Clanging far away.
Sometimes it whizzes nearer,
And then it seems to say
Whooooooooo!   Get out of my way!
Whooooooooo!   I'm in a hurry,
Whooooooooo!   Can't stop today,
Whooooooooo!   Get out of my way!

Low whistles — boo-oo-oom, boo-oo.
Shrill whistles — tree-e-e-e-t.
I listen to the whistles
From my window on the street.

THE STATION

The station is a busy place,
With miles and miles of trains,
That run all day and every night
And even when it rains.

There're lots and lots of people there,
With bags and boxes too,
And lots of men to carry them,
All dressed alike in blue.

And when you hear the whistle blow,
Along there comes a train,
And everyone calls out goodbye,
And kisses me again.

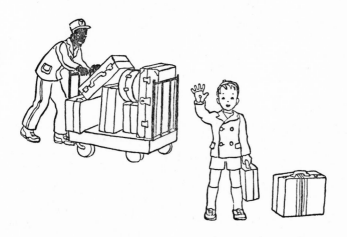

IF YOU LOOK AND LISTEN

If you stand at the station and look down the tracks,
Way, way down the tracks, past the signal tower,
To where the shining steel rails seem to come together,
If you look as far as ever you can,
Way, way down the tracks,
You can see a little black something.

If you stand at the station and listen and listen,
Above the noise of the telegraph clicking,
Click click click-click click-click click click,
Above the noise of the men with the freight,
Bumping it, thumping it down on the platform,
If you listen and listen with both your ears,
Way, way down the track,
You can hear something puffing.

What is it coming so fast, so fast,
Growing bigger and bigger as nearer it comes?
What is it coming so loud, so loud,
Louder and louder as nearer it comes?
What makes the singing sound on the rails,
The long steel rails that shine in the sun?
What is this monster rushing past,
Ever so long and loud?

PASSENGER TRAIN

When you ride on a train, a passenger train,
You walk down a long, long aisle,
With seats and seats and seats and seats
Along each side of the aisle.
You choose a seat that you like the best
And look out a window to East or West.
The train begins to move along,
The wheels begin to make a song
Speeding along on the long, long track —
Clicket-a-clacket, a-clacket, a-clack.
   Go the wheels of the passenger train.

When you ride on a train, a passenger train,
You sit on a high straight seat,
You look to see if this is a train
With a sort-of-a-shelf for your feet.
You put your feet on this sort-of-a-shelf
And you settle back to enjoy yourself.
And trees fly by, and the telegraph poles
The woods and fields, the valleys and knolls,
As you rush along the long, long track,
And their wheels sing their clickety clack,
   When you ride on a passenger train.

When you ride on a train, a passenger train,
You suddenly come to a town,
And a house and a house and a house and a house
Slip by as you're slowing down.
And the passenger station comes in sight,
The train stands still while you alight,
Then it disappears down its long, long track,
With its wheels still singing the clickety-clack
   Of a hurrying passenger train.

James S. Tippett

ENGINE

I wonder if the engine
That dashes down the track
Ever has a single thought
Of how it can get back.

With fifty cars behind it
And each car loaded full,
I wonder if it ever thinks
How hard it has to pull.

I guess it trusts the fireman;
It trusts the engineer;
I guess it knows the switchman
Will keep the tracks clear.

TRAINS

Over the mountains,
Over the plains,
Over the rivers,
Here come the trains.

Carrying passengers,
Carrying mail,
Bringing their precious loads
In without fail.

Thousands of freight cars
All rushing on
Through day and darkness
Through dusk and dawn.

Over the mountains,
Over the plains,
Over the rivers,
Here come the trains.

AN ENGINE

An engine is a big thing,
Big and black, wide and high,
Big round boiler, great huge wheels,
A big gigantic engine.

An engine is a noisy thing.
Choo choo choo choo.   *Choo* choo choo choo
Puff puff puff.   Ding ding ding.
It makes a lot of noise.

An engine is a hot thing.
The fire inside is red hot.
The steam inside is boiling hot,
Hot enough to burn you.

An engine is a busy thing.
It pulls a long, long train of cars.
All day long it pulls a train.
Busy, busy engine.

An engine is a strong thing.
It pulls a heavy, heavy load.
The great huge wheels turn round and round.
It pulls a heavy load.

An engine is a fast thing.
It rushes fast along the tracks.
Clickety clickety clickety click.
"I'll get there quick!   I'll get there quick!
I'll get there quick!"

"FUNNY THE WAY DIFFERENT CARS START"

Funny the way
Different cars start.
Some with a chunk and a jerk,
Some with a cough and a puff of smoke
Out of the back,
Some with only a little click —
        with hardly any noise.

Funny the way
Different cars run.
Some rattle and bang,
Some whirrr,
Some knock and knock.
Some purr
And hummmmmm
Smoothly on
        with hardly any noise.

STOP–GO

Automobiles
In
  a
    row
Wait to go
While the signal says:
             STOP

Bells ring
Tingaling!
Red light's gone!
Green light's on!
Horns blow!
And the row
Starts
    to

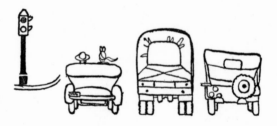

ROADS

A road might lead to anywhere —
  To harbor towns and quays,
Or to a witch's painted house
  Hidden by bristly trees.
It might lead past the tailor's door,
  Where he sews with needle and thread,
Or by Miss Pim the milliner's,
  With her hats for every head.
It might be a road to a great, dark cave
  With treasure and gold piled high,
Or a road with a mountain tied to its end,
  Blue-humped against the sky.
Oh, a road might lead you to anywhere —
  To Mexico or Maine;
But then, it might just fool you, and
  Lead you back home again!

RIDING IN AN AIRPLANE

Azzoomm, azzoomm loud and strong —
Azzoomm, azzoomm a steady song —
 And UP I went
 UP and UP
  For a ride
  In an airplane.

The machinery roarrrred
And whirrred
And jiggled my ears
Yet I
Just sat right
On a chair
Inside that airplane
And made myself
Stare
Out of a window.

There
Way down below
I saw autos
Scuttling along.
 They looked to me
 Like fast little lady bugs —
 So small!
And I saw houses
That seemed to be
 Only as big as match boxes —
  That's all!

But the strangest sight
Was when
We came to some clouds!

We stared *down*
Instead of *up*
To see them,
And they looked
Like puffs of smoke
From giant cigarettes.

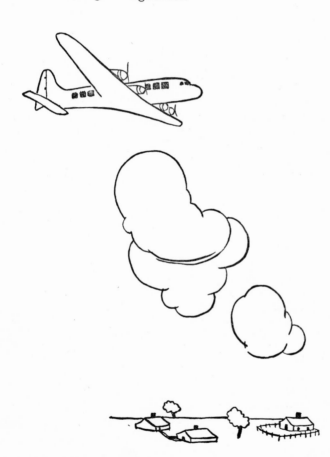

AEROPLANE

There's a humming in the sky
There's a shining in the sky
Silver wings are flashing by
Silver wings are shining by
Aeroplane
Aeroplane
Flying — high.

Silver wings are shining
As it goes gliding by
First it zooms
And it booms
Then it buzzes in the sky
Then its song is just a drumming
A soft little humming
Strumming
Strumming.

The wings are very little things
The silver shine is gone
Just a little black speck
Away down the sky
With a soft little strumming
And a far-away humming
Aeroplane
Aeroplane
Gone — by.

TAKING OFF

The airplane taxis down the field
And heads into the breeze,
It lifts its wheels above the ground,
It skims above the trees,
It rises high and higher
Away up toward the sun,
It's just a speck against the sky
— And now it's gone!

Ralph W. Bergengren

THE DIRIGIBLE

The only real airship
   That I've ever seen
Looked more like a fish
   Than a flying machine.

It made me feel funny,
   And just as if we
Were all of us down
   On the floor of the sea.

A big whale above us
   Was taking a swim,
And we little fishes
   Were staring at him.

BRIDGES

I like to look for bridges
Everywhere I go,
Where the cars go over
With water down below.

Standing by the railings
I watch the water slide
Smoothly under to the dark,
And out the other side.

FERRY–BOATS

Over the river,
Over the bay,
Ferry-boats travel
Every day.

Most of the people
Crowd to the side
Just to enjoy
Their ferry-boat ride.

Watching the seagulls,
Laughing with friends,
I'm always sorry
When the ride ends.

FREIGHT BOATS

Boats that carry sugar
And tobacco from Havana;
Boats that carry coconuts
And coffee from Brazil;
Boats that carry cotton
From the city of Savannah;
Boats that carry anything
From any place you will.

Boats like boxes loaded down
With tons of sand and gravel;
Boats with blocks of granite
For a building on the hill;
Boats that measure many thousand
Lonesome miles of travel
As they carry anything
From any place you will.

BACK AND FORTH

Back and forth
go the ferries,
back and forth
from shore to shore,
hauling people, trucks and
            autos,
back and forth
from shore to shore.

Back and forth
go the ferries,
either end
is bow or stern;
good old poky, clumsy fer-
            ries
they don't even
have to turn.

Back and forth
go the ferries,
Here's a freighter!
There's a barge!
Nosing through the harbor
            traffic,
tugs and steamers
small and large.

Back and forth
go the ferries;
anxiously
the captains steer
poking slowly through the
       fog bank,
coasting, bump!
into the pier.

Back and forth
go the ferries;
clang the bell
and close the door.
Streak of foam across the
     harbor.
Open gate,
They've reached the shore!

THE FOG HORN

Foggy, foggy, over the water,
Foggy, foggy, over the bay,
Foggy, so foggy the boats are like shadows
And how can they find their way?

Far away and over the water
Hear the voice of the fog horn say
"Whoo-oo-oo, I'm guiding you,
Boats that are out on the bay."

Foggy, foggy over the water,
Foggy, foggy over the bay,
And through the fog the boats go slowly
While the fog horn tells them the way.

BOATS SAIL ON THE RIVERS

Boats sail on the rivers,
And ships sail on the seas;
But clouds that sail across the sky
Are prettier far than these.

There are bridges on the rivers,
As pretty as you please;
But the bow that bridges heaven,
And overtops the trees,
And builds a road from earth to sky,
Is prettier far than these.

WHERE GO THE BOATS

Dark brown is the river,
Golden is the sand.
It flows along forever,
With trees on either hand.

Green leaves a-floating,
Castles of the foam,
Boats of mine a-boating —
Where will all come home?

On goes the river
And out past the mill,
Away down the valley,
Away down the hill.

Away down the river,
A hundred miles or more,
Other little children
Shall bring my boats ashore.

WATERS

Sprinkling
Wrinkling
Softly tinkling
Twinkling
Tiny brook,
Running
Funning
Hiding, sunning
Cunning baby brook,
Joins a grownup brook.
Dashing
Splashing
Sunlight flashing
Stony grownup brook
Joins the river
Broad smooth river
Deep as deep can be
Slower, slower, slower flowing,
Wider — Wider — Wider — growing,
Till it empties all its waters out
        into the great huge sea.
Rolling, — rolling, — tossing, — rolling,
Splashing waves forever rolling in the
        great wide sea.

about
the
seasons

Sara Teasdale

FEBRUARY TWILIGHT

I stood beside a hill
  Smooth with new-laid snow,
A single star looked out
  From the cold evening glow.

There was no other creature
  That saw what I could see —
I stood and watched the evening star
  As long as it watched me.

WISE JOHNNY

Little Johnny-jump-up said,
"It must be spring,
I just saw a lady-bug
And heard a robin sing."

THE CROCUS

The golden crocus reaches up
To catch a sunbeam in her cup.

DAISIES

The daisies running in the breeze
  Are 'fraid to go too far.
They stick their toes into the ground
  And stay right where they are.

I'd like to help them get away
  For a little bit of fun.
They may not be afraid if I
  Go with them for a run.

I get all set and count the start.
  I say, "One, two, and three."
I run and look back to make sure
  The daisies follow me.

They run a little way with me
  As if they'd like to play,
Then turn around with tossing heads
  And run the other way.

"We'd like to go with you," they say.
  "But we're rooted to the spot.
We can't get up and leave it —
  Do you really think we ought?"

I stand right still and make believe
  My toes are roots that grew.
"If you can't go one way with me,
  I'll go both ways with you."

THE DAY BEFORE APRIL

The day before April
    Alone, alone,
I walked in the woods
    And sat on a stone.

I sat on a broad stone
    And sang to the birds.
The tune was God's making
    But I made the words.

DANDELIONS

When I went out to play today
I found dandelions yellow and gay
And then when I came in tonight
The dandelions had turned to white.

They were so round and so soft, too,
I picked one up and blew and blew
And when I blew, why, do you know
The fluff came off — you try and blow!

SHORE

Play on the seashore
And gather up shells,
Kneel in the damp sand
Digging wells.

Run on the rocks
Where the seaweed slips,
Watch the waves
And the beautiful ships.

AT THE SEA–SIDE

When I was down beside the sea
A wooden spade they gave to me
To dig the sandy shore.

My holes were empty like a cup.
In every hole the sea came up,
Till it could come no more.

A SUMMER MORNING

I saw dawn creep across the sky,
And all the gulls go flying by.
I saw the sea put on its dress
Of blue mid-summer loveliness,
And heard the trees begin to stir
Green arms of pine and juniper.
I heard the wind call out and say:
"Get up, my dear, it is to-day!"

BED IN SUMMER

In winter I get up at night
And dress by yellow candle-light.
In summer, quite the other way,
I have to go to bed by day.

I have to go to bed and see
The birds still hopping on the tree,
Or hear the grown-up people's feet
Still going past me on the street.

And does it not seem hard to you,
When all the sky is clear and blue,
And I should like so much to play,
To have to go to bed by day?

SEPTEMBER

A road like brown ribbon,
A sky that is blue,
A forest of green
With that sky peeping through.

Asters, deep purple,
A grasshopper's call,
Today it is summer,
Tomorrow is fall.

DOWN! DOWN!

Down, down!
Yellow and brown
The leaves are falling over the town.

AUTUMN LEAVES

The leaves are dropping from the trees,
Yellow, brown, and red.
They patter softly like the rain —
One landed on my head!

But when the sleep of winter comes
They cuddle down to rest;
Then Mother Nature tucks them in
With snow as she thinks best.

AUTUMN FIRES

In the other gardens
  And all up the vale,
From the autumn bonfires
  See the smoke trail!

Pleasant summer over
  And all the summer flowers,
The red fires blaze,
  The grey smoke towers.

Sing a song of seasons!
  Something bright in all!
Flowers in the summer,
  Fires in the fall!

THE MIST AND ALL

I like the fall,
The mist and all.
I like the night owl's
Lonely call —
And wailing sound
Of wind around.

I like the gray
November day
And bare dead boughs
That coldly sway
Against my pane.
I like the rain.

I like to sit
And laugh at it —
And tend
My cozy fire a bit.
I like the fall —
The mist and all.

BABY SEEDS

In a milkweed cradle,
Snug and warm,
Baby seeds are hiding,
Safe from harm.
Open wide the cradle,
Hold it high!
Come Mr. Wind,
Help them fly.

James S. Tippett

AUTUMN WOODS

I like the woods
    In autumn
When dry leaves hide the ground,
When the trees are bare
And the wind sweeps by
With a lonesome rushing sound.

I can rustle the leaves
    In autumn
And I can make a bed
In the thick dry leaves
That have fallen
From the bare trees
Overhead.

COVER

Red leaves flutter,
Yellow leaves fall,
Brown leaves gather
Along a wall.

Brown leaves huddle
Against the gray
Stones some farmer
Set one way

Between two pastures.
Curled leaves keep
Any wall warm
When winter's deep.

BLACK AND GOLD

Everything is black and gold,
　Black and gold, tonight:
Yellow pumpkins, yellow moon,
　Yellow candlelight;

Jet-black cat with golden eyes,
　Shadows black as ink,
Firelight blinking in the dark
　With a yellow blink.

Black and gold, black and gold,
　Nothing in between —
When the world turns black and gold,
　Then it's Hallowe'en!

RIDDLE: WHAT AM I?

They chose me from my brothers:
"That's the nicest one," they said,
And they carved me out a face and put a
Candle in my head;

And they set me on the doorstep.
Oh, the night was dark and wild;
But when they lit the candle, then I
Smiled!

THANKSGIVING DAY

Over the river and through the wood,
  To Grandfather's house we go,
  The horse knows the way
    To carry the sleigh
Through the white and drifted snow.

Over the river and through the wood,
  Oh, how the wind does blow!
It stings the toes,
And bites the nose,
As over the ground we go.

Over the river and through the wood,
  To have a first rate play,
Hear the bells ring,
"Ting-a-ling-ling"!
Hurrah for Thanksgiving day!

Over the river and through the wood,
  Trot fast my dapple gray!
Spring over the ground,
Like a hunting hound!
For this is Thanksgiving Day.

Over the river and through the wood,
  And straight through the barnyard gate,
We seem to go
Extremely slow,
It is so hard to wait!

Over the river and through the wood —
  Now Grandmother's cap I spy!
Hurrah for the fun
Is the pudding done?
Hurrah for the pumpkin pie!

FIRST SNOW

Snow makes whiteness where it falls.
The bushes look like popcorn-balls.
The places where I always play,
Look like somewhere else today.

Dorothy Aldis

WINTER

The street cars are
Like frosted cakes —
All covered up
With cold snow flakes.

The horses' hoofs
Scrunch on the street;
Their eyelashes
Are white with sleet.

And everywhere
The people go
With faces TICKLED
By the snow.

SNOWSTORM

Oh, did you see the snow come?
  So softly floating down, —
White in the air, white on the trees,
  And white all over the ground!

It rattled gently on dry leaves;
  It tickled on my face;
And spread its thick, soft cover
  On every kind of place.

The autos standing in the street
  Had snowy tops and lights,
And even on my mummy's hat
  Was a big thick pile of white!

ICE

When it is the winter time
I run up the street
And I make the ice laugh
With my little feet —
"Crickle, crackle, crickle
Crrreeet, crrreeet, crrreeet."

THE SNOWMAN'S RESOLUTION

The snowman's hat was crooked
   And his nose was out of place
And several of his whiskers
   Had fallen from his face.

But the snowman didn't notice
   For he was trying to think
Of a New Year's resolution
   That wouldn't melt or shrink.

He thought and planned and pondered
   With his little snow-ball head
Till his eyes began to glisten
   And his toes began to spread;

And at last he said, "I've got it —
   I'll make a firm resolve
That no matter what the weather
   My smile will not dissolve."

But the snowman acted wisely
   And his resolution won
For his splinter smile was wooden
   And it didn't mind the sun!

STOPPING BY WOODS ON A SNOWY
EVENING

Whose woods these are I think I know.
His house is in the village though;
He will not see me stopping here
To watch his woods fill up with snow.

The little horse must think it queer
To stop without a farmhouse near
Between the woods and frozen lake
The darkest evening of the year.

He gives his harness bells a shake
To ask if there is some mistake.
The only other sound's the sweep
Of easy wind and downy flake.

The woods are lovely and dark and deep.
But I have promises to keep,
And miles to go before I sleep.
And miles to go before I sleep.

THE SNOWFLAKE

Before I melt,
Come, look at me!
This lovely icy filigree!
Of a great forest
In one night
I make a wilderness
Of white:
By skyey cold
Of crystals made,
All softly, on
Your finger laid.
I pause, that you
My beauty see:
Breathe, and I vanish
Instantly.

GALOSHES

Susie's galoshes
Make splishes and sploshes
And slooshes and sloshes,
As Susie steps slowly
Along in the slush.

They stamp and they tramp
On the ice and concrete,
They get stuck in the muck and the mud;
But Susie likes much best to hear

The slippery slush
As it slooshes and sloshes,
And splishes and sploshes,
All round her galoshes!

SNOW ON THE ROOF

When we came to school today,
There was snow on the roof,
Snow on the boxes,
Snow on the blocks,
Snow on the boards,
Snow on the stairs.
There was snow all around us,
But nobody cared.

We took the brooms and shovels,
We cleaned off the roof.
We shoveled off the boxes,
We swept off the blocks,
We shoveled off the boards,
We swept off the stairs.
Now we have snow all over us,
But nobody cares!

ICY

I slip and I slide
On the slippery ice;
I skid and I glide, —
Oh, isn't it nice
To lie on your tummy
And slither and skim
On the slick crust of snow
Where you skid as you swim?

WHITE FIELDS

(1)

In the winter time we go
Walking in the fields of snow;

Where there is no grass at all;
Where the top of every wall,

Every fence and every tree,
Is as white as white can be.

(2)

Pointing out the way we came,
Everyone of them the same —

All across the fields there be
Prints in silver filigree;

And our mothers always know,
By our footprints in the snow,

Where it is the children go.

SNOWFLAKES

Snowflakes falling through the air,
Falling, falling everywhere.

Twisting, turning, floating down,
Covering white the noisy town.

Roofs are laden, window edges,
Snow is sticking to the ledges.

All the streets are silent now.
Comes the whirring of the plow.

Clean behind it shines the track,
Cars are coming, click-a-clack.

People shoveling, piling snow,
Making clear the way to go.

Wagons crunch and autos whir,
Wheels that turn and never stir.

Children run and slide and tumble,
Snow all over, not a grumble.

Snowballs flying, dodge and run!
Here's a day of snowy fun!

WHEN SANTA CLAUS COMES

A good time is coming, I wish it were here,
The very best time in the whole of the year;
I'm counting each day on my fingers and thumbs —
The weeks that must pass before Santa Claus comes.

Then when the first snowflakes begin to come down,
And the wind whistles sharp and the branches are
       brown,
I'll not mind the cold, though my fingers it numbs,
For it brings the time nearer when Santa Claus comes.

"WHY DO THE BELLS OF CHRISTMAS RING?"

Why do the bells of Christmas ring?
Why do little children sing?

Once a lovely shining star,
Seen by shepherds from afar,
Gently moved until its light
Made a manger's cradle bright.

There a darling baby lay
Pillowed soft upon the hay;
And its mother sang and smiled:
"This is Christ, the holy Child!"

Therefore bells for Christmas ring,
Therefore little children sing.

THE FRIENDLY BEASTS

Jesus, our brother, kind and good,
Was humbly born in a stable rude;
The friendly beasts around Him stood,
Jesus, our brother, kind and good.

"I," said the donkey, shaggy and brown,
"I carried His mother up hill and down;
I carried her safely to Bethlehem town.
I," said the donkey, shaggy and brown.

"I," said the cow, all white and red,
"I gave Him my manger for His bed;
I gave Him my hay to pillow His head.
I," said the cow, all white and red.

"I," said the sheep with curly horn,
"I gave Him my wool for a blanket warm;
He wore my coat on Christmas morn.
I," said the sheep with curly horn.

"I," said the camel yellow and black,
"Over the desert upon my back,
I brought Him a gift in the wise man's pack.
I," said the camel yellow and black.

"I," said the dove from the rafters high,
"I cooed Him to sleep so He would not cry,
I cooed Him to sleep, my mate and I.
I," said the dove from the rafters high.

CRADLE HYMN

Away in a manger, no crib for His bed,
The Little Lord Jesus laid down His sweet head
The stars in the bright sky looked down where He lay —
The Little Lord Jesus asleep on the hay.

The cattle are lowing, the dear Baby awakes,
But Little Lord Jesus, no crying he makes.
I love Thee, Lord Jesus! look down from the sky,
And stay by my cradle till morning is nigh.

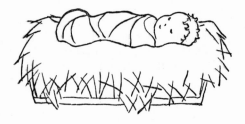

about
the
weather

Mary McB. Green

MIRRORS

Puddles in the street
Are mirrors at my feet
Shiny mirrors
Showing
Sky
And clouds
And trees
Still mirrors
Showing
Shimmering
Leaves.

Puddles in the street
Are mirrors at my feet
If I step
Carefully
I shall be
Very high
In the sky
With clouds
And trees
And shimmering
Leaves.
This mirror will not crack
If I step
Carefully
I only
Leave there
A ruffled track
Very high
In the sky
With clouds
And trees
And shimmering
Leaves.

IT IS RAINING

It is raining.

Where would you like to be in the rain?
Where would you like to be?

I'd like to be on a city street,
where the rain comes down in a driving sheet,
where it wets the houses — roof and wall —
the wagons and horses and autos and all.
That's where I'd like to be in the rain,
that's where I'd like to be.

It is raining.

Where would you like to be in the rain?
Where would you like to be?

I'd like to be in a tall tree top,
where the rain comes dropping, drop, drop, drop,
around on every side:
where it wets the farmer, the barn, the pig,
the cows, the chickens both little and big;
where it batters and beats on a field of wheat
and makes the little birds hide.

It is raining.

Where would you like to be in the rain?
Where would you like to be?

I'd like to be on a ship at sea,
where everything's wet as wet can be
and the waves are rolling high,
where sailors are pulling the ropes and singing,
and wind's in the rigging and salt spray stinging
and round us sea gulls cry.
On a dipping skimming ship at sea —
that's where I'd like to be in the rain;
that's where I'd like to be!

VERY LOVELY

Wouldn't it be lovely if the rain came down
Till the water was quite high over all the town
If the cabs and buses all were set afloat,
And we had to go to school in a little boat?

Wouldn't it be lovely if it still should pour
And we all went up to live on the second floor
If we saw the butcher sailing up the hill,
And we took the letters in at the window sill?

It's been raining, raining, all the afternoon;
All these things might happen really very soon
If we woke tomorrow and found they had begun,
Wouldn't it be glorious?   *Wouldn't* it be fun?

RAIN

Raining again
And raining again,
Freckles of rain on the
Window pane,
Pricks in the puddles
As bright as a pin
Stop and begin and then
Stop and begin:
John flats his nose on the
Window pane,
Watching and watching and
Watching the rain!
John can't remember
He's ever been
Any place but
Always in.

RAINING

It's raining, raining, raining,
And all the world is wet.
It rained last night, and now today
It's raining, raining, yet!

Drip, drip, drip, drip,
Leaking from the eaves,
Pattering, splashing, and tapping
On the roof and the tulip tree's leaves.

The quick little raindrops in puddles
Are dancing up and down;
Rivers rush down the gutters,
Foamy and dirty brown.

Drip, drip, patter and splash,
How fast the raindrops race, —
Running down the windowpane
Cold against my face!

RAIN

The rain is raining all around,
It falls on field and tree,
It rains on the umbrellas here,
And on the ships at sea.

"RAIN, RAIN, RAIN!"

Rain, rain, rain!
With my nose against the pane.
See the little raindrops hurry
Flurry-skurry in a worry;
Slip-and-sliding,
Drip-and-gliding,
In a never ending train.

MUD

Mud is very nice to feel
    All squishy-squash between the toes!
I'd rather wade in wiggly mud
    Than smell a yellow rose.

Nobody else but the rosebush knows
How nice mud feels
    Between the toes.

SWEEPING THE SKY

There was an old woman tossed up in a basket,
Ninety times as high as the moon;
And where she was going, I couldn't but ask it
For in her hand she carried a broom.
"Old woman, old woman, old woman," quoth I,
"Whither, O whither, O whither so high?"
"To sweep the cob-webs off the sky!"
"Shall I go with you?" "Aye, by-and-by."

THE WIND

I saw you toss the kites on high
And blow the birds about the sky;
And all around I heard you pass,
Like ladies' skirts across the grass —
O wind, a-blowing all day long,
O wind, that sings so loud a song!

I saw the different things you did,
But always you yourself you hid.
I felt you push, I heard you call,
I could not see yourself at all —
O wind, a-blowing all day long,
O wind, that sings so loud a song!

O you that are so strong and cold,
O blower, are you young or old?
Are you a beast of field and tree,
Or just a stronger child than me?
O wind, a-blowing all day long,
O wind, that sings so loud a song!

A KITE

I often sit and wish that I
Could be a kite up in the sky,
And ride upon the breeze and go
Whichever way I chanced to blow.

"WHO HAS SEEN THE WIND?"

Who has seen the wind?
Neither I nor you;
But when the leaves hang trembling
The wind is passing thro'.

Who has seen the wind?
Neither you nor I;
But when the trees bow down their heads
The wind is passing by.

CLOUDS

White sheep, white sheep,
On a blue hill,
When the wind stops
You all stand still
When the wind blows
You walk away slow.
White sheep, white sheep,
Where do you go?

BROOMS

On stormy days
When the wind is high
Tall trees are brooms
Sweeping the sky.

They swish their branches
In buckets of rain,
And swash and sweep it
Blue again.

FOG

The fog comes
    on little cat feet.

It sits looking
over harbor and city
on silent haunches
and then moves on.

THE WHIRL AND TWIRL

Like a leaf or a feather,
In the windy, windy weather;
We will whirl around,
And twirl around
And all sink down together.

just
pretend

OTHERWISE

There must be magic,
Otherwise,
How could day turn to night?

And how could sailboats,
Otherwise,
Go sailing out of sight?

And how could peanuts,
Otherwise,
Be covered up so tight?

GENERAL STORE

Some day I'm going to have a store
With a tinkly bell hung over the door,
With real glass cases and counters wide
And drawers all spilly with things inside.
There'll be a little of everything;
Bolts of calico; balls of string;
Jars of peppermint; tins of tea;
Pots and kettles and crockery;
Seeds in packets; scissors bright;
Kegs of sugar, brown and white;
Sarsaparilla for picnic lunches;
Bananas and rubber boots in bunches.
I'll fix the window and dust each shelf,
And take the money in all myself,
It will be my store and I will say:
"What can I do for you today?"

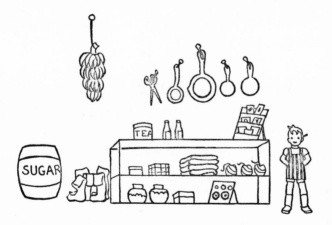

SOMEWHERE

Could you tell me the way to Somewhere —
   *Some*where, *Some*where,
  I have heard of a place called Somewhere —
  But know not where it can be.
        It makes no difference,
        Whether or not
        I go in dreams
        Or trudge on foot:
Would you tell me the way to Somewhere,
   The Somewhere meant for me.

There's a little old house in Somewhere —
   *Some*where, *Some*where,
A queer little house, with a Cat and a Mouse —
        A kitchen, a larder,
        A bin for bread,
        A string of candles,
        Or stars instead,
        A table, a chair,
        And a four-post bed —
There's room for us all in Somewhere,
   For the Cat and the Mouse and Me.

Puss is called *Skimme* in Somewhere,
   In *Some*where, *Some*where;
 Miaou, miaou, in Somewhere
 S–K–I–M–M–E.
        Miss Mouse is scarcely
        One inch tall,
        So *she* never needed
        A name at all;
        And though you call,
        And call, and call,

There squeaks no answer,
Great or small —
Though her tail is a sight times longer
Than this is likely to be:
FOR

I want to be *off* to Somewhere,
To far, lone, lovely Somewhere,
No matter where Somewhere be.
It makes no difference
Whether or not
I go in dreams
Or trudge on foot,
Or this time tomorrow
How far I've got,
Summer or Winter,
Cold, or hot,
Where, or When,
or Why, or What —
Please, tell me the way to Somewhere —
*Some*where, *Some*where;
Somewhere, *Some*where, *Somewhere*, SOMEWHERE —
The Somewhere meant for me!

A FAIRY WENT A–MARKETING

A fairy went a-marketing —
   She bought a little fish;
She put it in a crystal bowl
   Upon a golden dish.
An hour she sat in wonderment
   And watched its silver gleam,
And then she gently took it up
   And slipped it in a stream.

A fairy went a-marketing —
   She bought a colored bird;
It sang the sweetest, shrillest song
   That ever she had heard.
She sat beside its painted cage
   And listened half the day
And then she opened wide the door
   And let it fly away.

A fairy went a-marketing —
   She bought a winter gown
All stitched about with gossamer
   And lined with thistledown.
She wore it all the afternoon
   With prancing and delight,
Then gave it to a little frog
   To keep him warm at night.

A fairy went a-marketing —
   She bought a gentle mouse
To take her tiny messages,
   To keep her tiny house.
All day she kept its busy feet
   Pit-patting to and fro,
And then, she kissed its silken ears,
   Thanked it, and let it go.

THE PLAYHOUSE KEY

This is the key to the playhouse
  In the woods by the pebbly shore,
It's winter now; I wonder if
  There's snow about the door?

I wonder if the fir trees tap
  Green fingers on the pane,
If sea-gulls cry and the roof is wet
  And tinkle-y with rain?

I wonder if the flower-sprigged cups
  And plates sit on their shelf,
And if my little painted chair
  Is rocking by itself?

FOREIGN LANDS

Up into the cherry tree
Who should climb but little me?
I held the trunk with both my hands
And looked abroad on foreign lands.

I saw the next door garden lie,
Adorned with flowers, before my eye,
And many pleasant places more
That I had never seen before.

I saw the dimpling river pass
And be the sky's blue looking-glass;
The dusty roads go up and down
With people tramping in to town.

If I could find a higher tree
Farther and farther I should see,
To where the grown-up river slips
Into the sea among the ships.

To where the roads on either hand
Lead onward into fairy land,
Where all the children dine at five,
And all the playthings come alive.

THE MOON'S THE NORTH WIND'S COOKY

The Moon's the North Wind's Cooky,
He bites it day by day,
Until there's but a rim of scraps
That crumble all away.

The South Wind is a baker,
He kneads clouds in his den,
And bakes a crisp new moon — that greedy
North . . . Wind . . . eats . . . again!

NIGHT MAGIC

The apples falling from the tree
   Make such a heavy bump at night
I always am surprised to see
   They are so little, when it's light;

And all the dark just sings and sings
   So loud I cannot see at all
How frogs and crickets and such things
   That make the noise, can be so small.

Then my own room looks larger, too —
   Corners so dark and far away —
I wonder if things really do
   Grow up at night and shrink by day?

For I dream sometimes, just as clear,
   I'm bigger than the biggest men —
Then Mother says, "Wake up, my dear!"
   And I'm a little boy again.

THE WHITE WINDOW

The Moon comes every night to peep
Through the window where I lie:
But I pretend to be asleep;
And watch the Moon go slowly by,
— And she never makes a sound!

She stands and stares! And then she goes
To the house that's next to me,
Stealing by on tippy-toes;
To peep at folk asleep maybe
— And she never makes a sound!

Rose Fyleman

HAVE YOU WATCHED THE FAIRIES?

Have you watched the fairies when the rain is done
Spreading out their little wings to dry them in the sun?
    I have, I have! Isn't it fun?

Have you heard the fairies all among the limes
Singing little fairy tunes to little fairy rhymes?
    I have, I have, lots and lots of times!

Have you seen the fairies dancing in the air,
And dashing off behind the stars to tidy up their hair?
    I have, I have; I've been there!

SOME ONE

Some one came knocking
  At my wee, small door;
Some one came knocking,
  I'm sure-sure-sure;
I listened, I opened,
  I looked to left and right,
But nought was there a-stirring
  In the still dark night;
Only the busy beetle
  Tap-tapping in the wall,
Only from the forest
  The screech-owl's call,
Only the cricket whistling
  While the dewdrops fall,
So I know not who came knocking,
  At all, at all, at all.

THE BEST GAME THE FAIRIES PLAY

The best game the fairies play,
  The best game of all,
Is sliding down steeples —
  (You know they're very tall).
You fly to the weathercock,
  And when you hear it crow
You fold your wings and clutch your things
  And then let go!

They have a million other games —
  Cloud-catching's one,
And mud-mixing after rain
  Is heaps and heaps of fun;
But when you go and stay with them
  Never mind the rest,
Take my advice — they're very nice,
  But steeple-sliding's best!

WHO'S IN?

"The door is shut fast
And everyone's out."
But people don't know
What they're talking about!
Says the fly on the wall,
And the flame on the coals,
And the dog on his rug,
And the mice in their holes,
And the kitten curled up,
And the spiders that spin —
"What, everyone's out?
Why, everyone's in!"

THE SUGAR–PLUM TREE

Have you ever heard of the Sugar-Plum Tree?
'Tis a marvel of great renown!
It blooms on the shore of the Lollipop sea
In the garden of Shut-Eye Town;
The fruit that it bears is so wondrously sweet
(As those who have tasted it say)
That the good little children have only to eat
Of that fruit to be happy next day.

When you've got to the tree, you would have a hard time
To capture the fruit which I sing;
The tree is so tall that no person could climb
To the boughs where the sugar-plums swing!
But up in that tree sits a chocolate cat,
And a gingerbread dog prowls below —
And this is the way you contrive to get at
Those sugar-plums tempting you so:

You say but the word to that gingerbread dog
And he barks with such terrible zest
And the chocolate cat is at once all agog,
As her swelling portions attest.
And the chocolate cat goes cavorting around
From this leafy limb unto that,
And the sugar-plums tumble, of course, to the ground —
Hurrah for that chocolate cat!

There are marshmallows, gumdrops, and peppermint
  canes,
With stripings of scarlet or gold,
And you carry away of the treasure that rains
As much as your apron can hold!

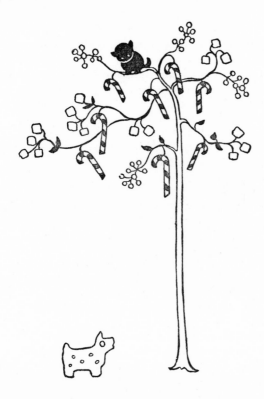

So come, little child, cuddle closer to me
In your dainty white nightcap and gown,
And I'll rock you away to that Sugar-Plum Tree
In the garden of Shut-Eye Town.

DIFFERENCES

Daddy goes a-riding in a motor painted gray,
He makes a lot of snorty noise before he gets away;
The fairies go a-riding when they wish to take their ease,
The fairies go a-riding on the backs of bumble-bees.

Daddy goes a-sailing in a jolly wooden boat,
He takes a lot of tackle and his very oldest coat;
The fairies go a-sailing, and I wonder they get home,
The fairies go a-sailing on a little scrap of foam.

Daddy goes a-climbing with a knapsack and a stick,
The rocks are very hard and steep, his boots are very
            thick;
But the fairies go a-climbing (I've seen them there in
            crowds),
The fairies go a-climbing on the mountains in the clouds.

THE LITTLE ELF

I met a little Elf-man, once,
Down where the lilies blow.
I asked him why he was so small,
And why he didn't grow.

He slightly frowned, and with his eye
He looked me through and through.
"I'm quite as big for me," said he,
"As you are big for you."

THE WEATHER FACTORY

Just as soon as summer's done,
Such a flit and flutter!
In the weather factory
Such a clip-and-clutter!

Nuts are begging, "Send us frost!"
In a month or so,
Children will be saying, "Ah,
If 'twould only snow!"

So the little weather folk
Dash around and scurry;
Everybody with a job,
Working in a flurry.

"Winkle, Twinkle, mix the frost.
Hoppy, grind the hail.
Make icicles, Nip and Tuck —
Thousands, without fail!

Tippy, start the flake machine
Quickly, and remember —
Twenty million tons of snow
Needed by November.

Whipper, Snapper, hurry up!"
Soon as autumn's come,
In the weather factory
Things begin to hum.

just
for
fun

HIDING

I'm hiding, I'm hiding,
And no one knows where;
For all they can see is my
Toes and my hair.

And I just heard my father
Say to my mother —
"But darling, he must be
Somewhere or other;

Have you looked in the INKWELL?"
And Mother said, "Where?"
"In the INKWELL," said Father.   But
I was not there.

Then "Wait!" cried my mother —
"I think that I see
Him under the carpet."   But
It was not me.

"Inside the mirror's
A pretty good place,"
Said Father and looked, but saw
Only his face.

"We've hunted," sighed Mother,
"As hard as we could
And I AM so afraid that we've
Lost him for good."

Then I laughed out aloud
And I wiggled my toes
And Father said — "Look, dear,
I wonder if those

Toes could be Benny's.
There are ten of them.   See?"
And they WERE so surprised to find
Out it was me!

THE BACKWARDS BOY

There's a funny thing in Funny Town —
It's a backwards boy who's upside down.
His feet are where his head should be;
And there is this that puzzles me:
If his head is always on the ground,
Is it flat instead of round?
And when he says "Yes," does he nod his head,
Or does he wiggle his toes instead?
When he wants some food to eat,
Does he take it with fingers or with feet?
I've pondered this with puzzled frown:
Does he button his overalls up — or down?

Alas, that we should never know
How the answers to these questions go!
We might as well just give it up.
This backwards boy — I made him up!

ELETELEPHONY

Once there was an elephant,
Who tried to use the telephant —
No! No! I mean an elephone
Who tried to use the telephone —
(Dear me! I am not certain quite
That even now I've got it right).

Howe'er it was, he got his trunk
Entangled in the telephunk;
The more he tried to get it free,
The louder buzzed the telephee —
(I fear I'd better drop the song
Of elephop and telephong!)

Nancy Byrd Turner

OLD QUIN QUEERIBUS

Old Quin Queeribus —
  He loved his garden so,
He wouldn't have a rake around,
  A shovel or a hoe.

For each potato's eyes he bought
  Fine spectacles of gold,
And mufflers for the corn to keep
  Its ears from getting cold.

On every head of lettuce green —
  What do you think of that? —
And every head of cabbage, too,
  He tied a garden hat.

Old Quin Queeribus —
  He loved his garden so,
He couldn't eat his growing things,
  He only let them grow!

THE OWL AND THE PUSSY CAT

The Owl and the Pussy cat went to sea
In a beautiful pea-green boat:
They took some honey, and plenty of money
Wrapped up in a five-pound note.
The Owl looked up to the stars above,
And sang to a small guitar,
"O lovely Pussy, O Pussy, my love,
What a beautiful Pussy you are,
> You are,
> You are!
What a beautiful Pussy you are!"

Pussy said to the Owl, "You elegant fowl,
How charmingly sweet you sing!
Oh! let us be married; too long we have tarried:
But what shall we do for a ring?"
They sailed away, for a year and a day
To the land where the bong-tree grows,
And there in a wood a Piggy-wig stood,
With a ring at the end of his nose,
> His nose,
> His nose,
With a ring at the end of his nose.

"Dear Pig, are you willing to sell for one shilling
Your ring?"   Said the Piggy, "I will."
So they took it away, and were married next day
By the Turkey who lives on the hill.
They dined on mince and slices of quince,
Which they ate with a runcible spoon,
And hand in hand, on the edge of the sand,
They danced by the light of the moon,
> The moon,
> The moon,
They danced by the light of the moon.

THE LOBSTER QUADRILLE

"Will you walk a little faster?" said a whiting to a snail.
"There's a porpoise close behind us and he's treading on
    my tail.
See how eagerly the lobster and the turtles all advance!
They are waiting on the shingle — will you come and
    join the dance?
Will you, won't you, will you, won't you, won't you
    come and join the dance?
Will you, won't you, will you, won't you, won't you come
    and join the dance?

"You can really have no notion how delightful it will be.
When they take us up and throw us, with the lobsters
    out to sea!"
But the snail replied, "Too far, too far!" and gave a
    look askance —
Said he thanked the whiting kindly but he would not
    join the dance.
Would not, could not, would not, could not, could not
    join the dance.
Would not, could not, would not, could not, could not
    join the dance.

"What matters it how far we go?" his scaly friend replied.
"There is another shore, you know, upon the other side.
The further off from England the nearer is to France —
Then turn not pale, beloved snail, but come and join
    the dance.
Will you, won't you, will you, won't you, won't you join
    the dance?
Will you, won't you, will you, won't you, won't you join
    the dance?"

SOMERSAULTS

Bunny turned somersaults;
    It was a surprise
To the ivory elephant
    With glossy, glassy eyes.

Somersaults . . . somersaults,
    Once and once again,
Until the ivory elephant
    Had counted more than ten.

Bunny told the elephant,
    I'm happy I'm not you . . .
You can't turn a somersault,
    Not even one or two."

And the elephant said,
    "Mercy, don't be such a prig,
I could turn a *million*
    If my nose weren't quite so big."

prayers

Mrs. E. R. Leatham

A CHILD'S GRACE

Thank you for the world so sweet,
Thank you for the food we eat,
Thank you for the birds that sing,
Thank you, God, for everything.

A PRAYER

Father, we thank Thee for the night
And for the pleasant morning light,
For rest and food and loving care,
And all that makes the world so fair.
Help us to do the things we should,
To be to others kind and good,
In all we do, in all we say,
To grow more loving every day.

NOW I LAY ME

Now I lay me down to sleep,
I pray thee, Lord, my soul to keep;
Thy love stay with me through the night
And wake me with the morning light.   Amen.

FOR THURSDAY

Dear Lord, we give thanks for the bright silent moon
And thanks for the sun that will warm us at noon.
And thanks for the stars and the quick running breeze,
And thanks for the shade and the straightness of trees.

PRAYER FOR A CHILD

When it gets dark the birds and flowers
Shut up their eyes and say goodnight,
And God who loves them counts the hours,
And keeps them safe till it gets light.
Dear Father, count the hours tonight
While I'm asleep and cannot see;
And in the morning may the light
Shine for the birds, the flowers and me.

"BLESS MY FRIENDS"

Bless my friends, the whole world bless,
Help me to learn helpfulness;
Keep me ever in thy sight:
So to all I say goodnight.

ACKNOWLEDGMENTS

WE WISH TO THANK the following publishing houses for their helpful cooperation and to make the following acknowledgments:

To W. Collins Sons & Co., Ltd., for permission to use "Who's In" by Elizabeth Fleming.

To D. Appleton-Century Co., Inc., for "The Little Elf" from *The St. Nicholas Book of Verse* by John Kendrick Bangs, published by D. Appleton-Century Co., Inc.

To The John Day Company, Inc., for "Stop-Go" from *I Like Automobiles* by Dorothy Baruch, reprinted by permission of The John Day Company, Inc.

To Doubleday, Doran & Company, Inc., for "Night Magic" from *Hearts Awake* by Amelia Josephine Burr, copyright, 1919, by Doubleday, Doran & Co., Inc.; for "The Ice-Cream Man," "The Playhouse Key," and "General Store" from *Taxis and Toadstools* by Rachel Field, copyright, 1926, by Doubleday, Doran & Co., Inc.; for "Have You Watched the Fairies?," "Differences," "The Best Game the Fairies Play," "A Fairy Went A-Marketing," and "Very Lovely" from *Fairies and Chimneys* by Rose Fyleman, copyright, 1920, by Doubleday, Doran & Co., Inc.; for "The Dentist" from *The Fairy Queen* by Rose Fyleman, copyright, 1923, by Doubleday, Doran & Co., Inc.; for "Mice" from *Fifty-One New Nursery Rhymes* by Rose Fyleman, copyright, 1932, by Doubleday, Doran & Co., Inc.; for "Regent's Park" from *Gay Go Up* by Rose Fyleman, copyright, 1929, 1930, by Doubleday, Doran & Co., Inc.; and for "The Blackbird" from *Kensington Gardens* by Humbert Wolfe, courtesy of Doubleday, Doran & Co., Inc.

To E. P. Dutton & Co., Inc., for "Bridges," "Galoshes," "Icy," "Milk in Winter," "Stars," "Snowstorm," "Under the Ground," "Little Bug," and "Raining" from *Stories To Begin On* by Rhoda W. Bacmeister, by permission of E. P. Dutton & Co., Inc., publishers and copyright owners; and for "Snow on the Roof," "Aeroplane," "I Listen to the Whistles," "There are So Many Ways of Going Places," "My Bed," "Other Children," "Seesaw," "Work Horses," "Little Black Bug," "The House of the Mouse," "If I Were a Little Pig," "Tiger-Cat Tim," "Grandfather Frog," "Jump or Jiggle," "Mirrors," "The Backwards Boy," and "It is Raining" from *Another Here and Now Story Book* by Lucy Sprague Mitchell, by permission of E. P. Dutton & Co., Inc., New York, publishers and copyright owners.

To Harcourt, Brace & Company, Inc., for "The Weather Factory" from *Magpie Lane* by Nancy Byrd Turner, copyright, 1927, by Harcourt, Brace & Company, Inc.

To Harper & Brothers. Acknowledgment is hereby made to Harper & Brothers for permission to use "Cat" and "Rabbits" by Dorothy Baruch; for permission to use "My Zipper Suit," "The Mitten Song," "Five Years Old," "Sneezing," and "First Snow" from Marie Louise Allen's *Pocketful of Rhymes*; and for permission to use "Autumn Woods," "Freight Boats," "Ferry-Boats," "Trains," "Engine," and "Sunning" by James S. Tippett.

To Henry Holt & Co., Inc., for "Fog" from *Chicago Poems* by Carl Sandburg, published by Henry Holt & Co.; for "Some One" from *Peacock Pie* by Walter de la Mare and "Softly, Drowsily, Out of Sleep" from *A Child's Day* by Walter de la Mare, both published by Henry Holt & Co., Inc.; and for "The Pasture" and "Stopping by Woods on a Snowy Evening" from *The Collected Poems of Robert Frost* by Robert Frost, published by Henry Holt & Co., Inc.

To Houghton Mifflin Company, for permission to use "Rain" from *A Pocketful of Posies* by Abbie Farwell Brown.

To Alfred A. Knopf, Inc., for "The Snail" reprinted from *Flying Fish* by Grace Hazard Conkling, by permission of and special arrangement with Alfred A. Knopf, Inc., authorized publishers; and for "Little Brother's Secret" reprinted from *Poems* by Katherine Mansfield, by permission of and special arrangement with Alfred A. Knopf, Inc., authorized publishers.

To J. B. Lippincott Company, for "Animal Crackers" reprinted from the section "Songs for a Little House" in *Poems* by Christopher Morley, by permission of J. B. Lippincott Company; for "Little Snail" reprinted by permission from *Poems by a Little Girl* by Hilda Conkling, copyright, J. B. Lippincott Company, publisher; for "Mrs. Peck-Pigeon" reprinted by permission from *Over the Garden Wall* and "Down! Down!" reprinted from *Joan's Door*, both by Eleanor Farjeon, copyright, J. B. Lippincott Company, publisher.

To Little, Brown & Company, for "Eletelephony" from *Tirra Lirra* by Laura Richards, "The Owl and the Pussy Cat" from *Nonsense Books* by Edward Lear, and "The Dirigible" from *Jane, Joseph, and John* by Ralph Bergengren, all reprinted by permission of Little, Brown & Company.

To The Macmillan Company, for "The Elephant" from *Pillicock Hill* by Herbert Asquith; for "The Lobster Quadrille" from *Alice in Wonderland* by Lewis Carroll; for "Roads" and "A Summer Morning" from *Pointed People* by Rachel Field; for "An Explanation of the Grasshopper," "The Little Turtle," and "The Moon's the North Wind's Cooky" from *Collected Poems* by Vachel Lindsay; for "Shore" from *Menagerie* by Mary Britton Miller; for "Back and Forth" from *Manhattan Now and Long Ago* by Mitchell and Lambert; for "Boats Sail on the Rivers," "The Postman," "Brown and Furry," "The City Mouse," "Who Has Seen the Wind?," and "Clouds" from *Sing Song* by Christina G. Rossetti; for "White Fields" and "The White Window" from *Collected Poems* by James Stephens; for "Autumn Fires," "My Shadow," "The Swing," "The Cow," "The Wind," "Rain,"

"At the Sea-Side," "Bed in Summer," "Where Go the Boats," and "Foreign Lands" from *A Child's Garden of Verses* by Robert Louis Stevenson; and for "February Twilight" from *Stars Tonight* by Sara Teasdale; all by permission of The Macmillan Company, publishers.

To Robert M. McBride & Company, for "Otherwise" reprinted from *The Coffee Pot Face* by Aileen Fisher, by permission of the publisher, Robert M. McBride & Company.

To G. P. Putnam's Sons, for "Brooms," "Hiding," "Rain," "Little," "The Goldfish," "Feet," "Hands," "Naughty Soap Song," "Riddle: What Am I?," "Winter," and "Ice" from *Everything and Anything* by Dorothy Aldis, courtesy of G. P. Putnam's Sons.

To Charles Scribner's Sons, for "The Sugar-Plum Tree" and "Why Do the Bells of Christmas Ring?" reprinted from *Complete Poems* by Eugene Field, published by Charles Scribner's Sons.

To The Viking Press, Inc., for "The Snowflake" and "Somewhere" from *Bells and Grass* by Walter de la Mare, copyright, 1942, by Walter de la Mare; for "The Woodpecker" and "Milking Time" from *Under the Tree* by Elizabeth Madox Roberts, copyright, 1922, and 1930; for "For Thursday" from *A Little Book of Prayers* by Emilie Fendall Johnson, copyright, 1941, by Emilie Fendall Johnson and Maude and Miska Petersham; for "Daisies," "Little Lady Wren," "Woodpecker with Long Ears," "Shoes," and "Robin" from *In and Out* by Tom Robinson, copyright, 1943, by Tom Robinson; all by permission of The Viking Press, Inc., New York.

To The Willis Music Company, for "The Friendly Beasts" from *Songs for the Nursery School* by J. Pendleton MacCartney, by permission of The Willis Music Company, copyright owner.

To the Yale University Press, for "Cover" by Frances Frost, reprinted from *Hemlock Wall*, Vol. XXVII in the *Yale Series of Younger Poets*, by permission of Yale University Press.

We also wish to thank and make acknowledgment to the following:

To Marjorie Barrows for "The Cricket" reprinted by permission of the author and *Child Life Magazine*.

To Dorothy W. Baruch for permission to use "Barber's Clippers," "Lawn-Mower," "Merry-Go-Round," "Funny the Way Different Cars Start," and "Riding in an Airplane" from *I Like Machinery* published by Harper & Brothers.

To Marietta W. Brewster for permission to use "Dandelions."

To Josephine Bouton for "The Station" and "Autumn Leaves" reprinted by special permission from *Poems for the Children's Hour* by Josephine Bouton, copyright, Milton Bradley Company.

To Eleanor A. Chaffee for "The Cobbler" reprinted by permission of the author and *American Junior Red Cross News*.

To Edwina Fallis for permission to use "September" and "Wise Johnny."

To Aileen L. Fisher for "Somersaults" and "The Snowman's Resolution," both reprinted by permission of the author and *Child Life Magazine*.

To Lois Lenski for permission to use "Tall People, Short People."

To Margaret Morrison for permission to use "I'm the Police Cop Man."

To Edith Newlin Chase for permission to use "The New Baby Calf," "The Fog Horn," "Passenger Train," and "Waters."

To Seumas O'Sullivan for permission to use "The Milkman."

To Lillian Schulz Vanada for permission to use "Fuzzy Wuzzy, Creepy Crawly."

To Muriel Sipe Ross for permission to use "Good-Morning."

To Eunice Tietjens for permission to use "Moving."

To Nancy Byrd Turner for permission to use "Old Quin Queeribus" and "Black and Gold."

To Sara Ruth Watson for permission to use "Bouncing Ball."

To Marjorie Seymour Watts for "New Shoes," reprinted by special permission of the author, from *Poems for the Children's Hour* by Josephine Bouton, copyright, Milton Bradley Company.

To Roberta M. Whitehead for permission to use "An Engine" and "If You Look and Listen."

To Dixie Wilson for "The Mist and All" reprinted by permission of the author and *Child Life Magazine*.

In some cases where poems have not been acknowledged, we have searched diligently to find the sources and to obtain permission to use the poems, but without success.